MW01600276

SELF MADE MIRACLES

By
Patricia Holmes
Copyright 1994

23284 Two Rivers Rd.
Basalt, CO 81621

CONTENTS

PICTURES

I.
INTUITIONS

There were many times when I felt that I should do something but I let my thinking interfere with my feeling. I'm not referring to emotional feelings but to a notion, a sense. If I had responded to the feeling, that small nudge, intuition or whatever you choose to call it, things would have been better. It began with small events.

Those small events were so frequent that I started writing about them. They were things I felt like doing but did not do because my reasoning talked me out of it. Later I found that if I had followed my feeling it would have saved me some inconvenience. Whenever I let my thoughts overrule my feeling, I learned I should have followed the feeling. At first the events were so insignificant that they simply would have made my life a little bit easier or less inconvenient. One of the first things I wrote, after several events had occurred, was as simple as when I was at work and got up from my desk to go to the ladies room and I felt that I should take my purse with me. I asked myself, why? I'm just making a quick trip to the ladies room. When I got there I found that I needed lipstick, a comb or maybe there was a vending machine that I wanted to use and I had no coins with me. So, I should have taken my purse with me when I felt I should rather than thinking about it and reasoning that I didn't need it.

Another time I sat a storm window on the ground and leaned it against the house at a substantial angle. As I did that it occurred to me that the window was going to break. I didn't need the window anymore so I felt that it wouldn't be a great loss if it broke, so rather than put it away in the garage where I knew it would not get broken, I increased the angle at which it was leaning. I reasoned that at that increased angle it would not fall over. When I was in the house I heard a sound that could have been something breaking. I knew it could not be the window because I had adjusted the position against the house so it would be impossible to fall and break. My curiosity got the better of me. I went outside to check on it. You guessed it. It was broken. How a breeze or wind or whatever could have gotten behind it and forced it forward I do not know. What I do know is something told me not to rest it there. My feeling was that I did not care if it broke. So it did. Now when I get those feelings I try to believe in them and think about what I really want and then take the time to make a plan for what I really want. Sometimes I find that I don't know what I want.

One time while I was watching my son's ball game it occurred to me that, sitting where I was, I was going to get hit by a ball. It was not a maybe like I might get hit. It was like the window. I was going to get hit. I thought about what I should do. I wanted to be close so I could see the game well and I had a good seat in comparison to where other people were sitting. It seemed pretty stupid to give up my seat to take another one behind people where I could not see as well. You guessed it again. I got hit by a ball. It was a child's game and I was not hurt but I did get hit.

Another time I was eating a tuna sandwich at my desk. I had a skirt on that required costly dry

Self Made Miracles

cleaning. I thought, You're going to drop something on your skirt. I started processing information. If I do drop something on my skirt I'm going to have to make a trip to the cleaners and I won't have the skirt in my closet to wear when I want it. Then I'll have to make another trip to the cleaners to pick it up and it will also cost me money. If I heed this message I can avoid all that inconvenience. So, I pulled the wastebasket out from under my desk, bent way forward in my chair and centered my head and shoulders over the middle of the basket. I felt really silly in that position until a chunk of tuna dropped from between the slices of bread into the center of the basket. I wanted to tell someone but no one else would have appreciated the whole scenario like I did.

I know other people experience similar things. I was driving on an expressway one day when I was not in a rush to get to where I was going. I saw a car on the shoulder of the road and a short way ahead of it was a young woman walking with a gas can in her hand. I believed she would feel comfortable taking a ride from a woman like myself so I pulled to the side of the road and offered her a

Intuition

ride. We talked about where she was from and then she told me that at the last exit she felt like she should have pulled off the highway to get gas. The fuel gauge was broken so she could not rely on it. She rationalized that she had not driven enough miles to use the fuel she had in the tank. Instead of following her feeling she acted on her reason and ran out of gas. She said it was really strange that happened because just a couple of weeks earlier, in a snowstorm, her husband pulled off a main road to a side road. She had a feeling that he should not leave the main road. After taking the side road they got deeply stuck in the snow. It was hardly an inconvenience because someone with a four wheel drive vehicle and a chain came along right at that time and pulled them out. Similarly, I gave her a ride and she was on her way in no time. Maybe, like I, she too was being taught to heed her feelings.

II.
GUIDED ACTION

Then there was the day I took more money to work with me than I ever had on any other day. It was something that was contrary to my practice. I didn't have a feeling or thought about it. I simply did something that was contrary to my practice. That was the day my car overheated and I needed money to repair a radiator hose. Fortunately, when it overheated I was close enough to a house to get water to allow me to drive the car to a repair shop. After work someone from the shop came to get me, I paid for the repair and there was little inconvenience. Without that extra money I would have had to find someone to give me a ride home that night and then someone to take me to work the next morning and have someone else drive me to the repair shop the next day. Having the extra money helped me avoid a lot of inconvenience.

Another time a young woman told me about the events that took place before her mobile home exploded. She described the miracle that saved her and her daughter. The park where she lived was expanding. Construction workers were coming at 6 a.m. to do underground work to extend electrical and sewer lines. She had complained to the park manager that 6 a.m. was too early to allow the operation of heavy equipment. Her companion had prepared to leave for work and drove around the park to defrost his car windshield. He returned and told Laura he would take her to her mother's house for the day. She was somewhat resistant. She needed to shower and get dressed. He told her no, she could do that at her mother's house. She said she would need to wake her daughter and dress her. He told her to just grab her daughter's clothes and dress her at her mother's house. Laura yielded to his direction and left her home with clothes in hand for her daughter and herself. A minute and a half later the mobile home exploded. Construction workers had hit a gas line with a front end loader. How can one deny that force out there that directs us. Why would her boyfriend return to insist she leave while still in her night clothes? What is the explanation for those unusual things we do that, in this case, saved lives.

III.
WE GET WHAT WE NEED

As I look back, there were many times when I was given exactly what I needed at exactly the right time. When my father died there were so many coincidences and unusual circumstances that brought my sister, my children and I together that we all agreed there was some strange and powerful force working to bring us together.

I just happened to be at my desk the morning my sister called to tell me that my father had been admitted to the hospital with respiratory failure and only had hours to live. I had been scheduled to be out of the office that day. I was not down the hall or in someone else's office. I just happened to be at my desk. It was midmorning and if I wanted to see my father one last time I would need to go directly to the airport from work without going home. I called my son Bob, who just happened to be home because his car would not start that morning. His roommate just happened to be with him and he would take Bob to my house so he could pack a bag for me and bring it to me at the airport.

The airline reservations were another case of things working out. At first I was told that from Michigan to Georgia I would have to go to Charlotte, NC, then to Atlanta and then to Macon, Georgia. Then I was told I would have a layover in Dayton, Ohio. Then I was told it was going to cost $749. None of that happened. I got a flight directly to Atlanta and the cost was $500. No stops and no layover and not $749. My niece's husband picked me up at the Atlanta airport and drove me to Macon. We had a chance to get acquainted without anyone else in the car. My father died two hours before I got there. Had I known I would not see him alive I would not have flown to Georgia. He was going to be brought back to Michigan to be buried. It was my sister who needed someone to be with her to help with the decisions on the funeral arrangements. By sharing the decision making it reduced the emotional overload that accompanied the shock of his unexpected death. I had an opportunity to spend time with my niece and nephew, to meet my nephew's new wife and to see their new house. I

Self Made Miracles

saw my father at a viewing my sister had in Macon and I had a precious few minutes alone with him to say good-by.

My son Larry was working in Aspen, Colorado at the time. There were so many people flying in and out on the week-ends that it was necessary to have airline reservations far in advance. When he called for a reservation, there was one seat available. He told me about that several times because when he called the airline he just knew there was no chance of getting a last minute seat on a week-end flight. He said, "Mom, people are begging for seats. They are booked months in advance." He said he could not believe it when the voice on the telephone said there was a seat available.

The most unusual event happened at a shopping center in Michigan. It was the Tel-12 Mall where there is a parking lot that may be as large as ten acres. There are numerous entrances to the many stores inside. My sister and I stopped there to see if we could quickly find some shoes for her. We were on our way to the funeral home. We quickly found a parking spot and hurried into the Mall. Just after we entered and had not gone far we met my son Bob. He lived twenty miles from this Mall. We had not discussed when he would be at the funeral home but there we were at the exact same place at the exact same time. After we finished expounding on our unusual meeting he had another surprise. When he stepped out of his car in the parking lot his brother Larry was just getting out of the car next to him. Larry had just flown to Michigan and he and Bob had not even spoken to each other yet. They agreed to meet back at their cars in forty-five minutes. By then there were four of us meeting. For all of us to meet at the same place, at the same minute with no knowledge of what each other was doing was just too coincidental to not suspect there was some force working somewhere that brought us together. We all arrived at the funeral home together as a family.

Even though none of us planned it, we were put together. My son was in the right place at the right time to help me get to the airport. I flew to Georgia to be with my sister when she needed me even though I did not know she needed me. Larry got a next to impossible flight out of Aspen in time

11

Self Made Miracles

to attend the funeral. Bob and he met at the shopping Mall by parking next to each other at the exact same moment. My sister and I just happened to walk into Bob at the precise same moment he was walking by the shoe store. We were being drawn together and we had little to do with it.

IV.
THINGS I COULD NOT GET

On the other hand, there were things I tried to do that I could not cause to happen. Twice I tried to get a home equity loan to pay off some charge accounts to do some home improvements, etc. There was no problem with my credit or my application. All the necessary paper work was in the right place to be processed but on one occasion when I called the lending institution, the clerk could not locate my application. I called again and the person I needed to talk to was on vacation. I felt there was no big rush so I called back a few days later. She was not available. Another call. Finally, everything was in order for a closing but by then I had paid off the excess bills and decided the most urgent reason for the loan was no longer present so I canceled the application.

A few years later when interest rates were drastically reduced I applied for a home equity loan again. This time the appraisal was completed and the paper work went through but I had forgotten about a lien I had on the property. Try as I did I could not get the legal work done to get the lien lifted. Finally, the time limit expired and whatever was motivating me to get the loan was no longer urgent. That was twice I was not able to refinance my home. When I was ready to sell my house a few years later I realized that if I had a larger debt on it I would not have been able to pay off the balance with the down payment, which also meant I would not have been able to offer owner financing which I needed to complete the sale. The two attempts to refinance that did not happen were ultimately in my best interest.

Another time I felt I needed to put a roof over my horses stalls. The rain leaked through rotten shingles and wind blew in through the broken doorway. Try as I did, I could not get someone to give me an estimate for the cost to repair the building. I called and called. First one person and then another. They did not return my calls or they never showed up for appointments to look at the building. I just could not get someone there when I could show them what I needed to have done. It would

Things I Could Not Get

have been a considerable expense that I could not have easily afforded at the time. It seems the Lord, or whatever, would not allow me to take on that expense.

I described the problem to a man who I knew at work. He had just gotten a builder's license and offered to do the repair. I later learned that he did not look at the roof before he agreed to put on the new one. I bought the materials and he came with his helper one Saturday morning. What a disaster! He started laying the plywood on top of the old rotten shake shingles. A main beam was rotted and needed reinforcement. I told him the structure needed some straightening before the new roof would fit properly. He saw that he did not have the knowledge to straighten the underlying structure. The problem was that he was not willing to admit it. Instead, he started hollering at me. He called me names and threw things around in a rage. He said, "You're nothing but a cheap bum." I was totally unaware of how that statement came about. Where did he get the word bum? He was the one who gave me a price I was comfortable with. It was a gorgeous fall morning. The sun was shining and the temperature was perfect. The leaves were changing so they were in shades of gold and this man was hollering so that his words were defiling the beauty around us. On such a still day his words were probably carried to neighbors on all sides of my property. I was shocked. I was not about to be involved with someone who behaved like that. I finally told him he should stop working on the roof and he should leave. He continued to tell me I was a no good. I turned and calmly walked, adrenaline and all, back to my house. I was really churning. What in the world was happening? He could have just talked about the work and what he was willing or able to do but instead he went into this rage with repetitious name calling and throwing tools and screaming. Whew! No more barn roof for me. I was through with that endeavor.

No matter how diligent I was there were some things that simply would not happen. I am sure there are many examples that others could give of things they simply could not bring about. It can be extremely frustrating until we learn that if it is not happening it could be because it is not the best thing for that time.

Things I Could Not Get

Back to a more pleasant side with the stalls. The horses could avoid the worst parts of the leaking roof. What they really needed was protection from the winter wind. I needed to close the outside door to their stalls at night to keep the cruel west wind away from them. I answered an advertisement in the "County Press" singles column. A man called me and we agreed to meet at the local coffee shop. Every small town has a bakery or cafe where, in the morning, all the local businessmen congregate. Our town only had one morning coffee shop so we met there. He was impressed with me and I agreed to meet him again. He showed me his cabin in the woods, the seclusion of it and the privacy. I showed him where I lived and my horses. I apologized for the condition of the barn. The door was about to fall off because the overhead beam was rotted. He looked at it and saw where the problem originated and commented on how the problem could be resolved. He was a person who liked a challenge. He arranged to come over one day to fix the door. I did not ask for his help. He offered. The biggest need for protection of my horses was to shut out the wind. Some strange force brought this man to resolve the need. I answered his ad. He answered my need and we never saw each other again.

So, some things are effortless and other things are extremely difficult. The couple of pieces of plywood that were put on the roof kept the roof from falling in but a few years later I had to move the horses and then I didn't need the stalls anymore. I must remind myself that if things are not working despite my efforts, maybe I should just let it go and see what the universe has in mind for the situation. If, in spite of all you do it seems you cannot achieve what you are trying to do, sit back and know that your best interests are being served even if you don't know what that best interest is. What is best for you will work out.

V.
BE CAREFUL WHAT YOU ASK FOR

We do get what we ask for. I had a car that I wanted to sell. In my mind I was willing to sell it for what I owed on it. I was not willing to take a loss. Whatever I owed the bank at the time was what I would sell it for. I was not about to have the car sold and still be paying for it. I got exactly what I asked for. The car did not sell for six months. I had a lot of people look at it. A lot of people admired it and wanted it but it did not sell until I had the balance on the loan down to what the car was actually worth. Then a young man in the village where I lived came to me, made me an offer and said he had the cash to close the sale with him. What he had was the exact balance of the loan. I accepted his offer and the car was sold. I could have sold it six months earlier for that price and paid the difference on the loan but I got exactly what I asked for. I just had to wait six months.

To get what we ask for we first need to

know what we want. Many times I have heard people ask for what they really did not want. It goes like this. "I don't care if I don't do well on this exam because I can eliminate one test score." No one wants to do poorly on an exam. What that person is really expressing is anxiety or fear about not being well prepared for the test. They are trying to relieve some of the stress. What a person does when they say things like that or have thoughts like that, is to program themselves to do poorly. They let down rather than try their very best. Consequently, they do poorly.

For example, "I don't care if Jack doesn't call." If she didn't care she wouldn't feel the need to say anything. But, by saying she doesn't care that thought is like a negative affirmation. I don't care if Jack doesn't call. So Jack doesn't call. A more honest statement would be. I hope Jack calls. Those words would cause you to act in a way that would bring about what you really wanted to happen. Maybe you tell a friend that you hope Jack calls you. That friend may ask Jack if he has called you. He may say that he has not called but he has been meaning to and thanks for reminding him. Things

Be Careful What You Ask For

don't happen just because you alone are completely in control. It isn't just because you say I hope Jack calls that he calls. A chain of events that you are not aware of can happen because you expressed what you really wanted to happen. We get what we ask for.

When we really want something to happen in our lives and it is good for us it does happen. Sometimes we ask for things by wanting them very strongly. Those things we have the most emotion for are sure to happen. It seems just asking for something without emotion is an empty request.

To my great surprise one day I found myself divorced and faced with the realities of planning a single life for myself and my four children. What would I do to earn money to support us? Should I go to work at any job or should I look for a job as a career? Would I ever remarry? If so, when? If it was going to be soon I could take any job. If it was going to be a long time I would need a career type job. Be real, who would take on the hassle of living with someone's four young children. How would I ever deal with all the personal problems that I felt churning inside of me not to mention the children's needs. Separated at twenty-eight and divorced at thirty. There was a lot of life ahead of me but how could I ever handle five lives all at once. Where would priorities lie and how could I ever make all those decisions that multiplied with every day. I did not know how I was going to cope but I did not panic--at least not for too long at one time.

I knew I wanted to be prepared to provide a future for myself and for my children that would satisfy my image of what I wanted my life to be. As a young girl I had friends whose parents were professionals that had college educations. Their families seemed more prosperous than mine. Their parents seemed to have a better image of themselves. They were able to do things that my family did not do. I remember my mother telling me that my father was only a fireman and he didn't earn as much money as my girlfriend's father who was a dentist. I did not want to go without the things I wanted. Therefore, I decided that I needed a college education. There was a lot of emotion behind the desire to have a comfortable life. I was committed to a future that was not stressful or full of deprivation. I wanted my children to be provided for. I wanted them to be happy and to see their world as a good place to live.

I had a lot of emotion about not returning to work as a secretary. I had worked as a receptionist and as a secretary. I did not like being an instrument for someone else's needs. I wanted to be the operator. As a secretary I felt like a production machine. I typed letters. I took the words from my boss in shorthand and reproduced them on the typewriter. I had no idea what those letters were about. I had no idea what his job was. I had no idea what all the correspondence in the files was about. I did not like not understanding what was going on. Even though I had skills that could help get me a job I had strong emotions about not working in that capacity. Another employer could have included me in what everything in the office was about but then I may not have aspired to get a college education.

For a while I was attending college classes just to get out of the house, to meet with other women and to find some stimulating activity to keep me vital. When my husband and I separated I

Self Made Miracles

quickly realized that I would have to make some very important decisions about my studies. Classes could no longer be taken just for fun. They were about to become a very serious activity that involved important decisions about my future which would affect my family. I had accumulated only one semester's credits in my previous lack-a-daisical approach to college. Would my husband keep his job long enough for me to collect child support until I finished a degree? Should I play it safe and stay on a two year program and be ready for a job in two years even though I had come to realize that nursing was not going to satisfy me. I had to decide if I would transfer to a four year education program or play it safe and finish my two year nursing program. I worried, I cried, I became irritable, resistant to those who advised me and then went on to do what I felt ultimately would be best for my children and myself. I gambled on making it through a four year program before my husband lost his job and I lost the child support I depended upon. If I stayed with the two year program I would be a nurse and I could work for sure. If I didn't make it through the four year program I would not be qualified to be a teacher or a nurse.

Be Careful What You Ask For

I found a tremendous support group at the college I attended. It was a group that met once or twice a week. A guidance counselor sat in and we students who had a lot of stress in our lives came and unloaded our problems there. I also had a compassionate and understanding counselor who supported me in my decisions. How would I ever get through three more years of college with four children from one to nine years of age. I certainly did not have the answer to how I would do it but I did know what I wanted. There was strong emotion behind my desire to complete my college degree.

Along the way to getting what you want there is no promise of a rose garden. In fact, I was so exhausted at one point in my early college days I didn't even know I was suffering from exhaustion. A counselor from the support group I attended offered me his cottage if I felt I needed a place to go for a while. He must have been reading me well because shortly after that I accepted his offer. I felt I needed some uninterrupted time to study. I sent my children off in different directions and packed a bag of books and an overnight bag for me and drove to his cottage. I let myself in, spread my books out on the coffee table and stretched out on the couch. I felt my body relax like a balloon with the air being released. I fell fast asleep. I had arrived at about 4 p.m. When I woke it was light outside. I had arrived in the late afternoon. It should be dark I thought. I was totally confused. I looked around for a clock. The clock said 11:00. But it wasn't dark. It must be morning. Eleven o'clock! The day was half over. I had slept nineteen hours. Five hours less than a whole day. I didn't need to pack my clothes because I had never unpacked. I put my books away and went back home. I did better than get what I asked for. I got what I needed.

I had to go to court to fight for child support payments. I did not have a car. I had to leave home an hour and a half earlier than if I could drive to school. Where would I find babysitters? I could do nothing without a babysitter. I absolutely had to get to school. I had to have money. All those dilemmas were not problems that could be taken lightly. They had to be resolved. I was running wild for awhile. Then my father would say, "Quit and be a secretary. You can type and take shorthand." I did not want to be a secretary for the rest of my life. I wanted a

Be Careful What You Ask For

short work day so I could be home with my children and I wanted sufficient money to support us. I was determined.

It was when I had decided I would have to get a part time job that someone told me the state gave loans to students. I absolutely had to have more income. I went to the bank. As I told the bank officer my problem he said, "Sure we can give . . ." and I knew there was a God. He was up there somewhere smiling saying, "See, you can do it." I was so relieved I felt like crying right at the man's desk. As I got into the car I wanted to let the tears of joy and relief flow but I didn't want others to see me so I restrained myself again.

When you really want something with a passion and it will be good for you, forces occur that cause it to come about. After I graduated from the two year college, I transferred to a four year institution. I had an appointment with a student loan officer. He told me how much money I could borrow if I qualified. I gave him my budget of what it would cost me to live and there was a few hundred dollars difference between my need and the loan amount. He told me it didn't look like I had enough money to make it through the school year. I thought he was going to deny me the loan. A moment of panic hit. I quickly thought that there was a God and I could get through on the money I had plus the loan. A shot of adrenaline surged in me and then calmly the right words came out. "I did it last year Mr. B.. I know the figures don't balance but I've always come up with some way to get through the school year."

I could not tell you how I made it on the money I had. My children's shoes got more miles out of them than most manufacturers would dare to advertise. All summer my children thought I was a swell mother for letting them go barefoot. On Sundays I would tell them they only needed to suffer for an hour or so with tight shoes at church. They could take them off as soon as we got in the car to go home.

When my youngest son was two years old I looked for a nursery school for him. Today it would be called a day care. I looked around for places I could afford. I finally put him in the least expensive school which was also very close to the college I attended. I took him there one morning. I had never visited the school. It was in a church building. I walked him in and the place was quiet. There were other children there but there was no laughter, no noise. The lights were dim. I had a bad feeling. I left and I was extremely upset. I had just left one of the most valued things in my life at a place I did not feel good about. I felt a pain that I remember today. My education was not worth this. My son's life was more important. I knew of an expensive day care that was operated by a former junior high school coach. He was an extremely loving and caring man. I went there. I put my name on their waiting list and much sooner than they expected there was an opening for Bobby. I paid what was necessary. I think it was about half my income. But, of course, I made it financially anyway. Sometimes, for some strange reason, money just goes farther than it should.

Just as the financial aid officer had told me that the figures showed I would not be able to make it through the semester on what I had, my figures showed that I could not afford to spend as much money as I was on child care. I knew I could not leave him at the other school. I had to put him where I felt he would be cared for in a warm loving atmosphere. He was there for a year.

Then I realized that to get through my program sooner I would need to move to the main campus of the University of Michigan in Ann Arbor. Once I realized that I put my house up for sale, sold it and we moved. It happened that in Ann Arbor there was a nursery school that was government subsidized. I only paid what my income level allowed. It was much less expensive. I would be relieved of the expensive burden of the child care cost. This nursery school was even better than the one I left. There were fewer children in the classes and younger people with more energy worked there. They were exciting and outgoing. They read to the children every day. A man came with a guitar and played songs and sang to the children. I couldn't wait to hear what was going to happen each week. My son was taught to put away his toys. On his birthday he wore a crown and the cook made a birthday cake with his name on it. He was fed in the morning. I was kept informed of everything that

Be Careful What You Ask For

Moving day. Children 10, 8, 2, and 12 years old.

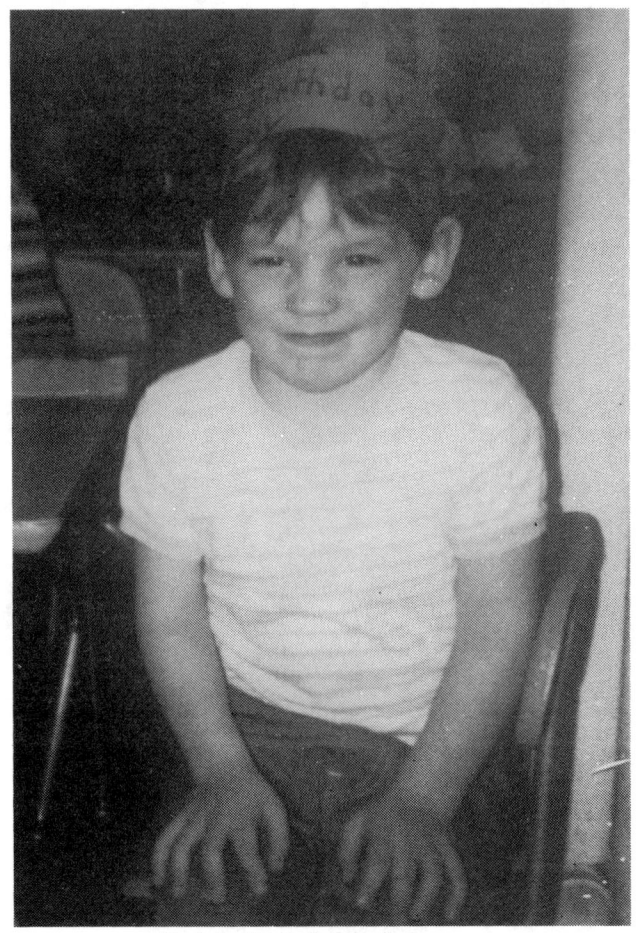

Bob's fourth birthday
at Perry Nursery School.

was going on at the wonderful Perry Nursery School. My prayers, wishes, hopes and dreams had been answered. My son was getting excellent care.

I met a lawyer who helped me get a wage assignment on my former husband's paycheck so I would always be sure of having the child support money. My stepmother convinced my father to buy me a car for the winter. Not having a car was an awful burden on my children. They had to walk a long way in the cold weather to go to school and back home again. I would wrap a scarf around their neck to be pulled up over their nose when the wind blew. Some days they would come home shivering.

When you are dedicated to causing something to happen all the unknown forces around you come to your aid when you most need them. It is not like you know things will work out because A is available and B will be available and C will happen therefore causing D, the goal, to be achieved. You simply need to believe that what you ask for will be granted even though you have no idea how it will happen. Emotion also needs to be present. I think Napoleon Hill described it as a burning desire.

VI.
I WILL GUIDE YOU

There was never enough money to meet my needs but strange gifts and guidance were near. One day, for some unknown reason, I went into the student union. It was not on my route to or from wherever I was going but I found myself reading a bulletin board. There was a notice of available fellowship money. It was the Lucy B. Elliot Fellowship. Money was available for women returning to school to complete their education. That day thoughts had been racing through my mind. How would I buy shoes for the children? They needed coats. I needed groceries. I didn't dare total what all my needs would cost. It was overwhelming. To get an application for the fellowship, this notice read, ask at the office. I was standing in front of that office. I walked in. I was given an application. The deadline to submit it was the next day. I sat down to submit it right then. It asked for an explanation of why I was applying for the money. Why? I hand wrote exactly what had been bothering me. There wasn't enough room to list all the places I had for the money to go. I wrote out my desperation for my children and for my education and our dire financial need. A few weeks later I got a letter that I had been awarded the Lucy B. Elliot Foundation money. It was $300. Hallelujah! I went to the store and bought groceries including pop and potato chips. I can remember excitedly coming into the house and telling the children we were going to have a party. We sat on the floor in the living room with the bag of potato chips and glasses for our pop. We talked about going shopping for shoes and new clothes. I never bought pop or potato chips. Those foods were too expensive and unnecessary. There was no room in my budget for extras. I had not tasted the sweetness of A & W root beer for such a long time. Some days, many days, there was only milk, sugar and cold cereal to eat but today was party time.

With God's help, are words that have been used often. What I accomplished after my divorce gave new meaning to those three words. As the student loan officer explained, on paper there was

Self Made Miracles

Growing up on cold cereal.

I Will Guide You

Graduation Day

Self Made Miracles

not enough money for me to meet my basic expenses. It was at those times that I had the sneaky feeling that some super force was keeping a very close eye on us. There was no simple formula. I did more with less than was humanly possible.

VII.
EMOTIONS MUST ACCOMPANY DESIRE

What I desire is delivered to me when I have strong feelings about it. After I graduated from college I married the man I had been dating for five years. He wasn't as nice a husband as he was a boyfriend. After five years of marriage I left. All I wanted was peace and tranquillity in my life. I wanted that so desperately that I was willing to give up all else to achieve it. My most tranquil moments were while I was riding my horse. When I decided to escape the pain in my life I went directly to the country where my horse lived.

I was working in a real estate sales office and a few people were talking about a house nearby that needed a lot of fixing. They were right! It needed a lot of fixing. The house was a weathered gray color from years of the elements pounding on it. I think I could relate. The kitchen ceiling was sagging so low that it was necessary to walk around the strips of lath protruding downward. The interior

39

was black with soot. There was no plumbing and no central heat. But, it had a nice floor plan. The kitchen was a good size and seemed like a room where people would gather. There were other older homes on the street that were well cared for and rested with a sense of stability.

Because of its neglected condition the price was very low. The seller wanted $5,000 plus the real estate commission and costs. That came to $6,400. I bought it. From there I proceeded to get a construction loan from the bank. I hired contractors and worked on it for months. The day came when it was ready to move into and it was January. At the right time, God had provided shelter and a job for me. He does not let us know ahead of time. He just takes care of needs at the precise moment. Sometimes it seems like the very last moment.

After I purchased the house my daughter came to visit me. "Mom stopped by, no one was here. Nice place. Love, Chris." Later in a waste barrel I found the top half of the paper bag with the first note. "Mom, stopped by, no was here—this is something else—couldn't find the house plus we had to go to the bathroom.

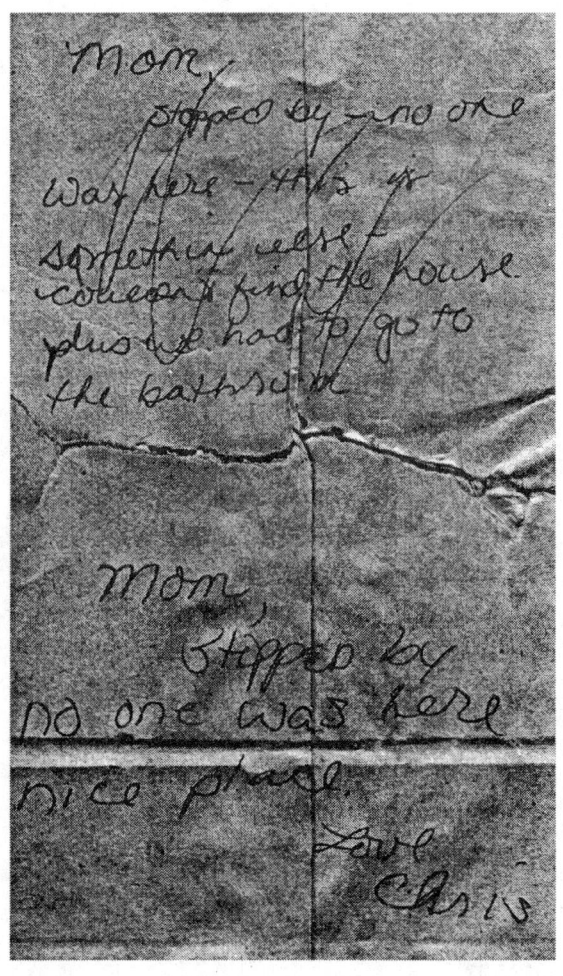

Self Made Miracles

Emotions Must Accompany Desire

My son brought one of his high school friends to visit. They were playing hide and seek when his friend opened a door that looked like a closet and stepped into an open pit. It was our dirt Michigan basement. He dropped about five feet straight down. Fortunately, it was fall and not spring. In spring the hole filled with water.

VIII.
ASK ONLY FOR WHAT YOU WANT, LEAVE THE HOW ALONE

I found another house that I wanted to renovate. It was a mile from where I lived and in a good area. It was a tall two story frame farm home with some apple trees in the center of the horseshoe drive. It had four out buildings to the rear of the property and an inoperative car on the front lawn. I mentioned the house to the broker I was working with. He knew the property was being handled by a lawyer in Florida and gave me his name and address. What luck, I thought. I had no success in reaching owners by going through the tax rolls. Now I had a responsible person who would most certainly answer my inquiry. The lawyer gave me the name and address of a local attorney who was handling the property. The owner had died two or three years earlier and the property was for sale. I met with the attorney and inspected the building. My experience had been that the inside condition was usually in a similar state as the exterior. It was true in this house. Plaster was cracked and falling from the wall, linoleum was worn and torn. The house was divided into three apartments and one of the apartments was extremely dirty. Untidy would not describe the condition of that apartment. I looked at the three units briefly. Yes, it was in poor condition. What price would I offer for it. I wanted it. I simply liked it. Intuition, a sixth sense, a feeling, it was one of those. I met with the lawyer again and was prepared to pay $35,000 to $39,000. As he talked, I realized that he probably had a very low valuation of this wreck. He probably had a very nice home and this place was the pits. As he spoke I tried to judge what price would not get me thrown out of his office. As he talked, the price in my mind kept going lower and lower. finally, he asked what I was prepared to pay for it. I, of course, asked what he wanted to sell it for. He being an astute business-man would not quote me a price. I, being an astute businesswoman had already picked up his clues as to what he thought the value was. Hesitantly, I offered $25,000. He agreed that was a fair price. I was ecstatic. We agreed on its value. He asked if I wanted to inspect it again. I declined the invitation telling him quite honestly that I was afraid to look too closely for fear I would change my mind. The sad ending to the price on this property was that when the attorney went to court to get the estate sale approved, an acquaintance of his said that he would pay $25,000 for that house. His offer had to be ten percent higher than mine to be considered so he offered $27,500. I then had to offer $30,250. He did not want to bid again so he cost me $5,250. It was still $5,000 to $9,000 less than I would have paid. The money was going to the cancer society which should have made me feel better.

I had $4,000. I needed more money for the down payment and to start repairs. How would I get the money? I did not have any personal friends who would loan me the money. I had already put a second mortgage on my other house. My former husband was not a possibility. My father always said no to everything. For weeks I tried to figure how I could get the money. Days before I was to close the sale I was at my wits end. I had not figured a way to get the money I needed. In desperation I drove fifty miles to my father's house for a visit. While I was there I told him of my plight. I knew better than to ask him for what I wanted on the telephone. When I asked him in person the answer was what I expected. No. His longtime girlfriend arrived about forty-five minutes later. He told her that I wanted to borrow $5,000. Something told me I should not ask for more than that. She said without hesitation, "Of course we can do that. You have $3,000 in such and such savings and I have $2,000 there. We can go there now and get the money before the bank closes," she said as she looked at the clock.

I could not believe what was happening. I held my breath for his answer. He mumbled something about the money and her opinion. She just said we had better do it now before the bank closes. I got in the back seat of their car. I think I was still holding my breath. I took shallow breaths waiting for the final outcome. What could go wrong? Would he change his mind at the last minute? Would he really withdraw the money? Would I really go home with the money I needed? We went to the drive-in window. Then he needed to go inside. I waited. I dared not to believe it would happen until the check was in my hand. He came back to the car, gave the check to her and she handed it to me! Oh, my Lord! I've got the money I need. I can buy that house. It really happened. I've got the house. I felt so strongly about buying that house and now it would happen. True, my father had never given me anything I asked for. But there was someone else who would. It was his money but she gave it to me.

I was getting adjusted to living in a new town and in my house when a friend came to invite me to come to the local tavern. I had been staying home and I was, as I look back, somewhat depressed. With great urging I went there. Some people were playing pool. They offered to show me how to play. I consented to a couple of mild drinks and before I knew it I was having fun. There was one particular man I was attracted to. He took time to show me how to play better pool. I saw him again after that night and he became important to me.

Soon my purchase of the second house was completed. Norman was a strong man and could easily do heavy work. I was strong willed but not so in the muscle department. As it worked out Norman and I enjoyed each others company socially and he gave to me profusely in the muscle department. Together we removed the asbestos siding and tar paper under it to expose the original lap siding on my house. What required great effort from me he did with vigor and ease. He scraped the entire house to prepare it for painting. He painted the high places and moved the ladder with a great show of strength. I painted the windows which were time consuming and detailed. I provided the paint and planned what to do next. After we finished the exterior of the house we started to work on the inside. In one kitchen we needed to take out the old plaster and put up new drywall. He got some of his friends to help and they took out the dirty broken plaster and lath. The room was filled with plaster dust. everyone was covered with filth and were walking on plaster and boards. It would have taken me a long time to do what they did in a few hours. Later we cleaned and painted another apartment. We pulled up old torn linoleum. I remember one night. We were trying to get some work finished so a renter could move in the next day. I was so exhausted that I sat in a folding chair to rest. I closed my eyes and

Self Made Miracles

Dryden Road House

fell asleep sitting up in the chair while he continued to finish what he was doing. He finished his work and woke me when we were to leave. He had tremendous energy and was apparently in my life at just the right time. I needed his strength and willingness to work. Not many men would work as energetically as he did on a building that was not their own. God, that higher power, or whatever helped me get the building and Norman helped me rebuild it. Norman was His gift to me. I truly enjoyed the hard work and the urgency of it. It was one step at a time. First, the decision to buy, then the purchase, then the repair. I did not know how, I just knew what I was going to do. The how would be resolved later. Our relationship lasted just a few months. It seems it was just long enough to get lots of work done and then he moved away. We continued to have a deep regard for each other and kept in touch now and then.

I had a burning desire to own that house. One person gave me the check for the purchase and another brought the muscle. I did not know she would be responsible for getting me the money or did I know he would be there to help. I was learning

Self Made Miracles

that you need to stick with what you feel and let the rest work itself out, because it will.

IX.
UNUSUAL ANSWERS

My childhood dream had been to live on a farm. I thought I had to marry a farmer to do that. But that was not true. A person who rented an apartment in my house had ordered some baby chicks through the mail. Can you imagine baby chicks in the post office? He didn't ask me if he could put chickens in the outbuilding. He just did it. When he moved away he left the chickens. For awhile they were roaming eating bugs and whatever chickens peck at on the ground. There were about four or five of them. Eventually, I realized they were mine as the renter did not return for them. I set a container of water out for them. Then I went to the feed store. I had to ask what to feed them. I grew up in the city. I had no idea what chickens ate. The people there were very helpful. They asked if they were laying hens. I didn't know so I bought scratch and mash. The scratch is a mixture of corn and oats that is cracked into small pieces. The laying mash is in powdered form. This was the beginning of my farming adventure. I learned the difference in appearance between roosters and hens. I put up boxes for the hens to lay eggs in but they rarely did. They preferred to make their own nests in the barn somewhere. I let them range free. I loved seeing them around the yard. They were white and a beautiful contrast to the green grass. Finding the eggs was not so easy. Looking for eggs was like Easter morning everyday. I got such a good feeling when I went to this property with the chickens roaming free. Predators eventually eliminated some of my chickens. I attempted to pen them to keep them safe. The pen didn't have green grass and they were confined. I couldn't enjoy watching them when they were fenced in so I let them roam. I could identify with the need to range free.

I really liked getting fresh eggs. There was a difference between my fresh eggs and store bought ones. The yolks were a golden color from the corn I fed them. The flavor was wonderful. My boys said that if they couldn't have our home grown eggs they didn't want eggs from the store. When there was only one or two of my chickens left I told

Unusual Answers

a friend of mine that I wanted to get some more chicks but I didn't know where to get any. He had some in his garage. He told me I could have his chickens. I asked if they were laying hens and he said they were. I accepted his offer and he delivered his chickens to me in the fall of the year. When the weather got cold I didn't get any more eggs. I fed them laying mash and I put fresh straw on the ground to keep them warm. I asked everyone I knew what I could do to get them to lay. Someone told me that when the days got shorter they didn't have enough daylight and that caused them to stop laying. If I put a light in the coop that might help. I arranged to run a long extension cord from the house to the chicken coop. I put a light on for them. I made trips to the coop to turn the light on and off. The snow came and still no eggs. One evening I drove into the yard after dark and saw the light from the coop reflecting on the snow. The spaces between the boards where the light shined through made yellow stripes on the snow. It was beautiful. The warm yellow glow on the cold white. Every day when I turned the light off and then on again I looked for eggs but all winter there were none. I had given up expecting them when in the spring I went to feed the chickens and found a fresh egg in a basket. Just when I had given up hope, there it was! Later, I learned that domestic chickens don't lay in the winter. That is why people butcher them and eat them. They don't pay their way in the winter. They just eat and don't give anything in return. I found a wonderful book, *The Chicken Book*, by Page Smith and Charles Daniels, 380 pages on chickens. I read it with great pleasure.

I had a rooster, I had hens and I had eggs. Why didn't I have babies? I learned that you need setting hens to get eggs to hatch. I had laying hens that produced eggs. Now I needed setting hens. I was discussing that with another renter and he just happened to have some setting hens at his mother's house. He would give me some of his. Someone left me the chickens. Someone else gave me more chickens. Now another person was giving me setting hens. God delivers whatever you have a yearning, a desire for. All this at no cost. I never asked for the first chickens but I did want to be a farmer and this was my beginning.

When I found one of the setting hens hidden

in the back of the barn spread out over her nest of eggs, I got so excited I could hardly stand it. I had noticed there was one less chicken in the yard for a while. I didn't know where she was. Was she dead? Did she just wander off? Then, there she was setting on a nest of eggs. I didn't know how long she had been there so I didn't know long it would be before the eggs would hatch. When I got near she would hiss and make me go away. If I tried to touch her she pecked at me. I eventually left her alone. How did she survive? Every time I peeked at her she was on the nest. I put food and water next to her but she didn't seem interested. I enjoyed watching her, checking on her, waiting for the big event. The anticipation was wonderful. It was when I gave up and thought she was just sitting on empty eggs that she delivered. I was out in the barn picking up and straightening when I saw her with baby chicks around. What a miracle. They were adorable. She clucked for them and they came running. When they chirped she knew where they were. I watched their communication. They had a system and it worked. She was so attentive. She spread her wings and could cover them all. They could hide between her wing and her body. I enjoyed my chickens so

Self Made Miracles

New chicks and I

58

very much. I felt such peace with them. I had not asked for chickens. I was dedicated to establishing tranquillity in my life. I never imagined that it would be delivered to me in the form of some left over chickens.

X.
INTRODUCTION TO PRINCIPLES

I became acquainted with a woman in the village where I lived who wanted to go to a Unity church to hear Og Mandino speak. He wrote, *The Greatest Salesman in the World*. A very dear friend of mine told me I should read that book while we were having a conversation about my career in real estate sales. I never did find the book, but as so often happens, the seed had been planted by his mention of it. The next step was meeting Fran. Then her desire to hear the author speak. It was December and the church was overflowing with people who had come to hear him. I benefitted by the experience and decided to return to the church in January for a weekly series called, Growth Through Goals, by Mike Wickett. I drove fifty miles to the church each Wednesday for the six or eight weeks of the series. It was there I learned about affirmations and imaging.

Introduction to Principles

For three years I had secluded myself in the small town of Metamora. I worked on my two houses, cared for my animals and held a job selling real estate in a depressed economic time. I was a substitute teacher at local schools to bring in some money. My life was on hold. I didn't have a plan. I had achieved what I wanted, peace. I didn't know what I wanted for my future. I had one son still in high school. I was so grateful for the tranquillity in my life that I hardly dared wish for more. When Mike gave out a blank sheet of paper with lines to be filled in with goals I was at a loss. I was not alone. Others had difficulty writing fifty things they wanted to be, achieve or have. We were encouraged to think big. Then others volunteered what they had on their lists. He soon had the room pulsating with enthusiasm. When one man said he wanted a body like Arnold Swartzeneger, the people roared with laughter and applause. It was with that encouragement that I dared to imagine a better life. One statement on our handout sheet was, What was I told as a child? That was easy to answer. Even though I was not conscious of its presence in my mind, I wrote that I was told I needed someone to take care of me. I looked at the paper belonging to the woman next to me. She had written the same thing in almost exactly the same words. I realized I had to let go of that idea.

One of the first affirmations I wrote, among others, was, "Money comes to me in the most unusual ways." I needed money quite seriously. I wrote this affirmation on a 3" x 5" card and put it on the bathroom mirror so every morning I would see it, read it and concentrate on it. I put another card like it in my purse to take out to read whenever I thought about it. Writing affirmations in the present tense as if what was wanted was already happening helped train me not to look for the how but to simply concentrate on what I wanted and let some other force take care of the how.

While I was home one day I saw my neighbor pass by the kitchen window on her way to the back door. This neighbor had never been to my house before and she was walking at a fairly quick pace. I opened the door, curious to learn what was on her mind. She had a thriving business in her home creating Victorian Christmas decorations. She also created other holiday and general occasion centerpieces. She recently began using taxidermy items in some of her expensive centerpieces. She was interested in buying some of my chickens to use in her centerpieces. My chickens had varied colors because they were crossbred and not pure Rhode Island Reds or Barred Rocks. Normally a laying hen sold for $3 or $4. I asked her what she thought she would pay for them and how many she wanted. When she told me she would pay $15 each I was shocked! Five times the usual rate? She was not sure how many she wanted so we went out to look at them. She found three that were suitably colorful and she felt that she did not want the expense of having to pay for more than three at the taxidermist. These chickens were not going to a cooking pot. They were going to be preserved. I sold them to her and had $45 in my pocket.

I had done nothing to get this money. It came to me. She knocked on my door and handed me $45. I did not offer to sell eggs or chickens to anyone. I never dreamed of money coming to me in this way. Just as the Lord takes care of the birds in the winter, so will he take care of you.

Self Made Miracles

I'm sure if you had a magic card in your possession that brought you money you would continue to keep it around. Naturally, I kept this card on my bathroom mirror and in my possession. The $45 was probably an introduction for me to believe in affirmations. What happened next was equally unusual. I moved into the three unit house I renovated. I lived in two of the units and rented one. People in the village knew I had apartments in the house and would occasionally tell someone who was looking for an apartment to see me. One day Debbie came to the door and asked to speak with me about a rental. She was working as a farm hand just a mile away and had living quarters provided with her job. She had a young son who would be starting school in the fall. Her former husband had the boy for the summer. For her to have him through the school year she needed to put him in a nearby school. For some reason the school district she lived in was not convenient or suitable so she needed an address in the school district I was in. She had discussed the situation with the principal of the school she wanted her son to attend and they were in agreement. She offered to rent an apartment or room in my house, pay for it and not use it! She simply needed the address. Of course I agreed. I showed her the upstairs and told her she could use it if she liked. I would move my bedroom furniture to the downstairs. No, she had a house and was not interested in using it. I quoted her a price that was half of what I charged for a full apartment. She paid me six months rent and went on her way.

Now, who among us would ever dream of asking in our prayers for someone to rent an apartment and not use it? Again, I was being shown that I did not have to have answers. I just needed to ask and trust and leave the details up to the universe.

This was not the end of money coming to me in unusual ways. A few weeks later Paul came to my door. He wanted to rent a room. He had been staying at his girlfriend's parent's home which was a few miles from my house. Her parents thought he should move out for the next few months before the two got married. He just wanted a sleeping room. He was polite, well-mannered and had a neat appearance so I considered his offer. I rented him a room for half the price of the entire apartment. Debbie had already paid for half the rent and now he was paying the other half. I had not advertised space to rent. I had not told anyone I wanted to rent any part of my house. I just read my affirmations and thought, Money comes to me in unusual ways. As it happened his job took him out of town sometimes for a week or two at a time. I rarely saw him and it was like he wasn't even there.

My use of affirmation cards and those highly unusual ways money came to me cannot be disputed. I certainly had no role in causing Debbie or Paul to bring me money in the ways they did. I didn't ask Arlene to buy my chickens. I began to believe that I could cause some of my needs to be filled by my thoughts and feelings rather than by running around frantically trying to be in control of how my needs would be met. I also learned that if my efforts were not causing what I wanted to happen to occur I had better sit back and let it go. I am the type of person who goes after what I want in a direct persistent manner. It was hard for me to sit back and let go.

My persistence in trying to get the roof on my horses stalls could be considered a lesson in backing off. The Lord probably said, I'm going to have to stop this woman from spending what money she has on what she thinks will protect her beloved horses. Then He sent a man to give me a bad experience so I would give up on the effort. Someone was sent to repair the door which would give them better protection than the roof. I don't have to work hard for everything I get. If I do the right things it will come knocking at my door. I just need to ask for what I want and the how will take care of itself.

By reading my affirmations I implanted what I wanted to happen in my mind, in my feelings, in my psyche. They were somewhere in my soul. What was important was that wherever they were, however they were, percolating about, they materialized in my life.

XI.
GRAF AFFIRMATION

I had peace in my home, serenity in my environ-
ment but the lack of income plagued me con-
stantly. My efforts to sell real estate were not
bringing me money. The substitute teaching was
barely enough money to buy groceries. I was busy
but I was not earning enough. My former husband
was foreclosing on my home because I had not paid
him the money I borrowed. I had used my home as
collateral for the loan. I was behind in my property
taxes and mortgage payments. I simply did not have
enough money to live on. I arranged for a meeting
with the assistant pastor at the church to learn what
I could do to correct my situation.

He asked me what I wanted. Just as God
would say to you in a dilemma, "What do you want
child?" I decided that I needed a long term solution
to the many immediate financial responsibilities
that I was unable to meet. I wanted a job that I

liked. I wanted to earn a steady income that I could rely upon. I wanted to work with people I respected and who I could trust. I wanted them to be friendly and cordial to me. In other words, I wanted a job that I liked and where those around me liked me. I was not there to see the pastor about a simple problem. I needed a career and money immediately! He listened to me. That is so important for a good counselor. He heard what my needs were and he helped me to fix them. He wrote out an affirmation and asked me if that covered everything. We discussed a few of the things I wanted to happen and then he rewrote it. He read it to me and then we talked about it again. I decided that I needed to be creative in my job. This is what we came up with. The right career now comes to me quickly and in peace where I can use my creative ability, surrounded by loving intelligent co-workers and where I receive an abundance of money for my services. He directed me to write this affirmation fifteen times a day for thirty days. He wrote it on a memo pad that was similar in size to a doctors prescription pad. The direction to write it fifteen times was similar to taking X number of pills for X number of days. I dated the prescription, oops, memo, and

Self Made Miracles

MEMO from JACK GRAF   March 8, 1984

The right career now comes to me
quickly and in peace where I can use
my creative ability, surrounded by loving,
intelligent co-workers, and where I receive
an abundance of money for my services.

15x. - 30 days -

DAY-TIMERS RE ORDER No 2472 — Printed in USA

70

Graf Affirmation

followed the doctors, pastors advice. I was dedicated to this affirmation. My back was against the
wall. I had to find a job that would pay me on a
regular basis. I did not have time to shop around. I
needed a direct connection and quickly. I wrote that
statement fifteen times a day. It took considerable
time, but each time I wrote it I began to visualize
myself having the right career come to me. I did not
know what the right career was but I came to
believe that the right career would come to me. I
could not afford to be shy. I wrote my affirmations
at the kitchen table where my boys could see what
I was doing. If they did not see me writing it they
could not have helped but see the writing around the
house. I was not about to write pages and immediately dump them in the wastebasket. That would
have been like throwing my wish away. I had pages
and pages of this affirmation everywhere. In the
kitchen, on my desk, in my bedroom. I could not sit
and write all fifteen at one time so I would put the
paper down and then pick it up again later. I began
to think that when elementary teachers used to have
students write sentences as punishment those
teachers may have actually been correcting the
behavior. I will not throw spit balls. I will not throw

71

spit balls. I will not throw spit balls. The right career now comes to me quickly and in peace—no anxiety, no begging for a job, no running place to place, no panic. Because I believed in the effectiveness of affirmations I believed I would receive what I asked for. I had never written anything as urgent or as comprehensive as this but all those smaller requests had prepared me for this larger request. Then the day came when I found myself driving to an interview.

I found an advertisement for an admissions representative at a business school. I called the telephone number and found there was going to be a group interview the following week. I had the day and time in my mind and I was going to attend to get more information about the job. I thought about what I would wear. During the week I thought about the position. I realized that it was a sales position and I did not want anything to do with sales. I needed a regular income but I did not want that job. If I did not want that job there would be no reason for me to go to the interview. Right? Wrong.

The day of the interview arrived. I found

myself putting on makeup. When I looked in the mirror I thought, what are you putting on makeup for? I never wore makeup during the day when I worked around the farm. Before I realized it I was in the car driving down the highway to the interview. I do not recall getting dressed, leaving the house or driving the country road to the main highway. When I was driving south to the interview I asked myself, what are you doing on this highway? You decided not to go to this interview. My car and I were headed there so I continued. I arrived at precisely the right time. I found the room and walked in with a very uninterested attitude. I had decided not to attend this interview. How was it that I was there? It was weird, spooky, kind of scary. Is that what people call guided? I had decided not to attend this interview but there I was.

As I left the room and walked down the hall to the exit I noticed a sign on the wall that said Chapin College. I would be interested in working in a college. I followed the arrow to the basement and looked around. The place was quite deserted. I looked into every vacant room. I heard some voices and then a woman appeared. I asked her where

Self Made Miracles

Chapin College was. She directed me to talk to the man behind the desk in the room she had just left. He informed me that he was writing the application for the creation of Chapin College. We had a nice talk in the setting I preferred, one to one. He said in the future they would be needing teachers and asked me to leave my resume with him. Meeting him was the reason I was at that interview. Later, he got a call from the director of the business school. She asked him if he knew anyone who could teach typing. He gave her my resume and she called me. I had listed on my resume that I typed and that I had been substitute teaching classes in typing and shorthand. When she asked if I would teach a typing class, I said "Yes."

When I met with the director, she gave me the typing book and the course outline and told me classes started in three days! Then I realized she was as much in a panic for a teacher as I was for a job. Some unusual forces acted upon me to get me to that group interview so I could meet Mr. Masterantonio, so he could recommend me to the director, so she could offer me a job I would accept. I'll never forget driving down the highway asking myself how I got there.

In the class I was teaching I was also learning. When a student asked me a question I would point to the explanation in their book. I would read it to them and then explain what it meant. I read it to them because I didn't know the answer without referring to the text book. I had to learn basic things. Directions would ask the student to set their machine for a 60 space line. If there are 72 spaces across a page or paper, subtract 6 spaces for a right margin and 6 spaces for a left margin. That leaves a 60 space line.

Then, the counting test for setting up columns. In high school I disliked counting spaces on a line to figure how to make charts and columns come out even. I am not a detail person and those assignments drove me right out of typing class. I would "eye ball" it and set margins that looked okay to me. If they were off by a space or two of being equal that was okay with me. Of course, it was not okay with the instructor. I took one year of typing when most business program students took two years. I do believe that whatever we refuse to learn comes back to us until we learn whatever we resisted. I was now teaching others how to set up columns. I had a great deal of compassion for those who struggled with those assignments.

After a few months the part-time position led to an offer of a full-time position teaching typing and job placement. I enjoyed scanning the help wanted advertisements, writing a student's name beside a job opening and bringing it to class. I was doing for them what Mike Wickett had done a year and a half earlier for the audience at his series. I helped the students see themselves in jobs that they earlier may not have considered. I told them how well they would do in their interviews, on their telephone inquiries and in their letters of inquiry. I supported them in what they wanted for themselves. As I scanned the newspaper one day I read a display ad placed by a community college. Among the positions was a placement specialist. That was what I was doing. I sat the paper aside and a few days later I thought that I should practice what I preach. Apply for everything that interests you. I was not earning very much money on my job. I called the college for an application, the deadline was near. I got a letter written and my son personally delivered it to the college. I got an interview. I was called back for a second interview. Before I left the second interview, I asked how many applicants were still being considered. Then I asked how many were women. The new job would be working with women who were low income and receiving assistance from Social Services. My feeling was that I needed some edge to put me before the other applicants. I think I asked a higher power for insight into what that deciding factor would be. Then I told the interviewer that I felt a woman would do a better job than a man in that capacity. A woman could relate to the female student's circumstances. Myself, with four children could relate to them very well. I was the only woman being considered. I got the job. When he apologized for the salary he didn't know that it was nearly double what I had been earning.

XII.
IMAGING

I learned about imaging at the Unity church. I cut out pictures of what I wanted in my life. My first collage of pictures included a woman in a business suit, a jet plane symbolic of travel, women enjoying coffee together symbolizing friendship, my horse and my car. Another picture was of a well-dressed woman getting out of a car with her head held high exuding self confidence. I would keep my serenity and build a career that also built my self esteem. Those images became imprinted on my mind so that even when I was not thinking about them they were there. All of those images materialized. I wore a suit to work. I traveled, I had friends, self esteem and confidence.

After a considerable period of time I realized that I had asked for the right man in my life who I felt had not been delivered. It was at a much later time after that when I realized none of my image pictures included men. Men had caused me considerable discomfort. My father ignored me. The father of my children was physically abusive and my second husband was emotionally abusive. No wonder I had no pictures of men around me. I had men in my life but they were there for pleasure. There was no one I would consider for a husband or life companion. Yet it seemed that according to my need there was a man there for me. When I needed to be treated with reverence someone was there. When I needed to be entertained there was someone there. When I needed a vacation to recharge, a companion was there. My feeling was that I didn't want a husband. My request was for the right man for me and that was what had been delivered according to my feelings not my thoughts.

After an inner struggle I got myself to look for pictures of men to create an image page. That was interesting. Would I look for pictures of suave businessmen? Maybe a handsome proper man? What appealed to me? Even though I liked athletic men the tennis player's looks were not my style. Soon enough I realized that the outdoor man was who I enjoyed looking at most. Polo players, men on horseback, the Marlboro man. The country club man was fine but my feelings were with the frontier type. As I looked at my collage of pictures there were some I simply had no positive feeling for when I looked at them. I found it difficult to look at this page that was tacked to my bedroom wall. I forced myself to complete this composite. More than once I found myself avoiding looking at it. A year or more later when all my men were on horseback and in the mountains I could enjoy looking at this image page. Then I realized I was looking at their backs. The Marlboro man was a front view and some were turned in their saddles but most were a back view. I enjoyed looking at them but they were not paired with a woman and my feeling was that I couldn't be happy living with them. I needed to be able to get away when they began mistreating me or before they began mistreating me. My second husband only seemed happy when I was unhappy. His purpose when he came home at night seemed to be to get me out of my good mood. Therefore, there were men in my life at the level I felt I wanted them. My thoughts told me I wanted a loving, caring partner but my feelings were for pleasurable experiences and for them to go away

Imaging

before the unpleasant treatment crept in.

Self Made Miracles

82

Imaging

I wanted a meaningful relationship with a man but I realized that my expectation was that there was no one out there for me. I really did not expect it to happen. My belief was contrary to my wish. I had to change my thinking to allow what I really wanted to happen. First, I timidly asked for a meaningful relationship. I got that. That wasn't really what I wanted. Then I asked for an affection-ate relationship. I got that. That wasn't really what I wanted. Then I asked for a romantic relationship. I got that. But that was not enough. What I really wanted was to have an emotional relationship. Now I was getting scared again. Dare I admit to myself that I wanted a loving relationship. Hank Hartmann had drawings in a local paper each week and one said: "I just want this." The illustration was of a person picking just one flower. "Why limit?" was the question from above. I needed to take a long look at some erroneous thinking.

Back to the affirmation cards and image pictures. I found pictures of men and women to-gether. Those went on my wall. When I looked at those pictures I imagined them having positive feelings toward each other. Then I imagined them

Self Made Miracles

actually enjoying each other. One step at a time I was bringing myself to believe that a man and woman could be happy together. Loving was going to take a little longer.

XIII.
WE DO GET WHAT WE DESIRE

Of course that higher intelligence gives us only what we can handle at our level of development. I was living at my 3½ acre farm with no animals. I was driving about thirty miles to work. I was isolated because once home from work I would busy myself there. I talked to no one. My children were grown and gone. It was a lengthy drive to attend any programs or weekly meetings so I didn't do that. I found after getting home I got more tired all the time. Then I realized that without my horses I had no one to touch or to love. I missed seeing them in the pasture. I missed feeding them in the morning. The fresh air always woke me and got me moving quickly. After work they were not waiting for me to feed them. This home didn't feel as good to me as it had before. Then I wanted better circumstances, wall to wall carpeting, a washer and dryer, lower heating bills. As I worked in my flower garden one day the thought occurred to me that I could have all of that without the expense of each item if I moved to an apartment.

In a couple of days I began looking. I found two that I liked. I rented my living quarters and moved within two months. It was all surprising to me. God grants wishes so easily. My wall to wall carpeting did not cost me a thousand dollars. I got a washer and dryer without giving up living space or having to pay for them. That winter I saved over a hundred dollars a month in heating costs. I was closer to people I knew so they could visit me and we could attend functions together. All these facets of my life that I was unhappy with were resolved as if someone had waved a magic wand. It was so easy.

I had been fascinated with underwater adventure probably since the TV programs Adventures in Paradise and Sea Hunt (1957-1961). I never allowed myself to wish for the opportunity to swim underwater like Gardner McKay or Lloyd Bridges. But the desire to experience that stayed inside of me, dormant. When I was in Hawaii I saw scuba lessons painted in large letters on a building. I thought, that is for me! I wanted to do that. I felt like it was possible. The feeling was released like a genie from a bottle sleeping all those years patiently waiting. I did not have the time to dive while I was in Hawaii but the feeling had been released. I had no idea how or when I would learn to scuba dive but the feeling, the desire was very strong. Within weeks a dear friend of mine said he wanted to experience scuba diving and would I be interested in taking the class with him. He would pay! Yes! Within weeks of my awakened desire we were enrolled and learning to dive. He absorbed all the costs! I didn't have to figure where I would get the money, how I would pay for it. It was all taken care of. It came so quickly without stress or strife. What I wanted so strongly came true. The ideas I held the strongest emotion for materialized first. My desire had not been supplanted by thoughts that I could not afford the cost. My thinking had not intruded on my feeling. I was in the water before my thoughts had a chance to tell me I couldn't do it.

I was certified in September 1989. It was one of the most exciting things I had ever done. We went to a gravel pit near my house for our qualifying dives. It was then I realized that when I drove by that site I used to think about it being a popular place to dive. I knew a man who said he and his son had been diving there. The idea of diving had been surfacing when I drove by that site but I never dreamed that I would be there diving. I had not allowed myself to dream. It wasn't until Hawaii that the genie, the desire, jumped out of the bottle.

When I went under water and relied on my self-contained breathing apparatus to sustain life for me, I was relying on faith of another kind. When I had to take my mouthpiece out of my mouth and give it to my buddy to breath from, I was relying on faith. When I calmly took it back, my faith was reaffirmed. When I felt the change in pressure cause me to sink, I called on my training to adjust my buoyancy. When I was surfacing and the change in pressure caused me to bounce upward I had to think about what to adjust to slow my assent. On the second day when my friend and I finished our last qualifying dive we were exhilarated. My boys had come to witness this event. They were truly proud and amazed by their mother. The look in their eyes was one of admiration and pride.

We Do Get What We Desire

My next desire was to dive in some warm water. I collected beautiful pictures of divers and made a collage to put on my bedroom wall. Every morning as I opened my eyes I looked at the beautiful tropical waters. Winter was approaching in Michigan and I did not think of ice diving as a pleasure sport. My friend did not want to continue diving. I didn't want to forget what I had learned but going south could be costly and I didn't know anyone else who dove. I had met a person earlier who dove and wouldn't you know, he called me. He was going to be in the Florida area and maybe Michigan. I had a free time share week available. We worked out a plan where we would meet in the Dominican Republic for my time share week. I had a coupon for air travel that would cover the cost of my flight to Miami. I could get to a warm water diving site with a minimum of cost and be with a person who I looked forward to seeing. He was the only person I knew who dived and we were headed for a wonderful experience together.

Another serendipitous experience occurred. My car broke down on the highway the following April. A towing facility was just opposite where it broke down. After it was towed to the garage I noticed pictures on the wall of unusual recoveries. Among those were pictures of people in scuba gear getting vehicles out of the water. After a few return trips for my car I wanted to meet whoever the diver was. I finally met the young man who owned the facility and had participated in the recoveries. After I returned from diving in the Dominican Republic I had a similar problem with my car and returned to have it looked at again. This time I told the owner that since I had seen him I had made seven dives. He invited me to go with him to test drive my car. It was then he invited me to dive with him and his friends in a month or so. Previously I had been furious that a car I had owned only three months had a mechanical problem and left me stranded on the highway fifty miles from home. How I got home is another story. But the repair shop was as near as a place could be and was owned by a scuba diver. We talked about his recoveries and his boat and diving ship wrecks. It was my good fortune that my car broke down and that I was directed to his facility to tow it.

In August I drove to Whitefish Point in the

We Do Get What We Desire

Michigan upper peninsula on the Lake Superior shore. The boat was more than forty feet long. He had invited his brother-in-law, a friend from Florida and he had his young son with him. When he said grace at lunch I knew I was in a good place. His friend was a scuba instructor and he took me for the first dive. It was exciting. I was a new diver and they were patient and caring. There wasn't much left of the ship Myron but I was at the bottom of Lake Superior at a hundred year old ship wreck. The next dive, I later learned, was called a bounce dive. I went down much deeper, touched the stern of the ship Vienna and was taken back up. The water was cold. I felt the thermocline change in temperature. I was excited by the depth, the quiet, the eerie nature that I experienced there. An astronaut said that deep diving was much like being in outer space.

How unusual this chain of events was. Hawaii where the idea got energy. Michigan where I got certified. Then meeting someone who dove and I experienced diving in the warmer tropical water. Then my car broke down at a place where I would meet another diver. Why? How? The more I dove the more I wanted to dive and people came to

91

Self Made Miracles

me to deliver just what I desired. The affirmation card, the image pictures on my bedroom wall, the desire, then the delivery. Was this how life delivered what I wanted for myself? When I pushed my desires aside I did not experience them. When I admitted what I wanted and allowed myself to feel strongly about what I wanted, it happened. It did not happen because I could buy it but because some strange force simply delivered it to me.

It was after I returned from my scuba vacation that I realized I had actually reproduced in life a picture that I had on my wall. The picture was of a man and woman snorkeling in the most beautiful blue water you could imagine. One day my friend and I had gone to an out-of-the-way beach where he did some free diving and I attempted to do the same. I looked at the ocean bottom through my mask and enjoyed the freedom of swimming in the quiet water out away from the beach. It was a duplicate of the picture on my wall. I had no intention of snorkeling nor had I ever heard of free diving. But, I experienced exactly what I had pictured for myself.

XIV.
MASTERMINDING

I joined a Master Mind group. That is a kind of prayer group of people who support each other in what they ask for themselves and for others. We followed the eight steps that Jack Boland from the Unity Church of Today outlined which were taken from the twelve step Alcoholic Anonymous program. After reading the steps each of us would tell the group what we wanted to have manifested in our lives and the lives of others we cared about. Then each member would repeat our requests back to us and tell us that they could see that happening for us. Somehow listening to someone else tell you that what you want is going to happen makes it more believable. I remember asking that my friend who was dying of cystic fibrosis be given courage and peace. When another member of the group told me that they believed he would experience the courage and peace that I wished for him, it made me feel better. When I arranged a research trip to Tahiti and

Self Made Miracles

I asked that it really happen, I could believe it was possible when they repeated my request back to me. Somehow listening to someone else tell me that what I wanted was going to happen made it believable.

The next week we would gather and report on the fulfilled requests. It seems when I asked for things out loud I was more aware when the request was granted. If I wanted the Dean to treat me more respectfully rather than being so confrontive, I recognized that my request had been answered when she spoke to me in a cordial manner as we passed in the hall. When I asked to be aware of erroneous thinking I would suddenly get an insight into some thoughts that were not working for me.

The hardest task was attempting to think bigger. I guess I had been pushing down good thoughts of good things because I didn't believe they would happen and I didn't want to be sad or disappointed. What good things did I want to happen? The time came at my college job when I no longer felt I was helping people. The supervisor did not want the department I worked in. The secretary had never done her job. My co-workers were unhappy and complaining. I was tired when I thought about going to work and I was tired when I came home. I had proven to myself that I could earn a substantial wage, own a nice car and live in a nice place. The question was, now what? My affirmation card read, "I have a nine month position. I have time to exercise, have fun, meditate, write, etc." My cards were asking for less hours on the job so I could enjoy other things. Then my job was terminated.

I could have never left that position on my own. I did not know what I wanted to do next. I applied to other colleges but my heart, emotion, was not in it. I was qualified for open positions but I never got an interview. Later I found affirmation cards that said, "I have summers off. I have time to take care of my physical and spiritual needs. I have a substantial passive income." Be careful what you ask for, you'll probably get it. I was laid off on the first of July. I had my summer off. I had time to take long walks for exercise. I began meditation and I had a passive income from unemployment compensation. I got what I asked for. I never imagined my passive income would be unemployment compensation.

It seems God was closing chapters in my life one at a time. Two years earlier my horses had each died. With their loss my country place was an unhappy place. When I looked into the pasture I felt a terrible sadness. My move to the apartment was a separation from my house and my country life. A dear friend of mine was ill and because I was not working I was able to see him several times a week. He died on his birthday November 4th, 1991.

My job had ended. I was obviously being directed to a new beginning. It was Thanksgiving and all of my four children and four grandchildren were together for the holiday. My son was home from Aspen, Colorado. Michigan was getting cloudy and gray in preparation for the winter. We talked about job opportunities in Aspen. I did not want a college job. I did want to be around happy people in a happy place. I was confident that my higher power was working for my highest good.

I now know that everything happens for the

Masterminding

best. I do not always know what that best is, but eventually it will be revealed. When I feel nudges or intuition I respond. I still sometimes must remind myself to listen-up, but I try my best to always go with the feelings. I am much more peaceful now when things don't work out. I truly believe it is because whatever did not work out was not best for me. I give thanks for the things that do work out and I know that what happens, happens at the best time. I try to relax and be open so that I will recognize opportunities as they arise. When doubts enter my mind I ask what do I want rather than what I don't want. I keep trying to raise my expectations to a higher level.

Good to me used to be the absence of pain or suffering. I had many good experiences that were pleasurable but my life track was a struggle against pain and suffering. It was only when my income was substantial, I had a reliable car and a comfortable lace to live that I reached the mean. No joy, no pain, just a plateau of comfort.

On my drive to Aspen I felt a wonderful peace that told me I was about to embark on a new

Self Made Miracles

adventure that would include pleasure. The avoidance of pain was behind me. I was about to reach a new level.